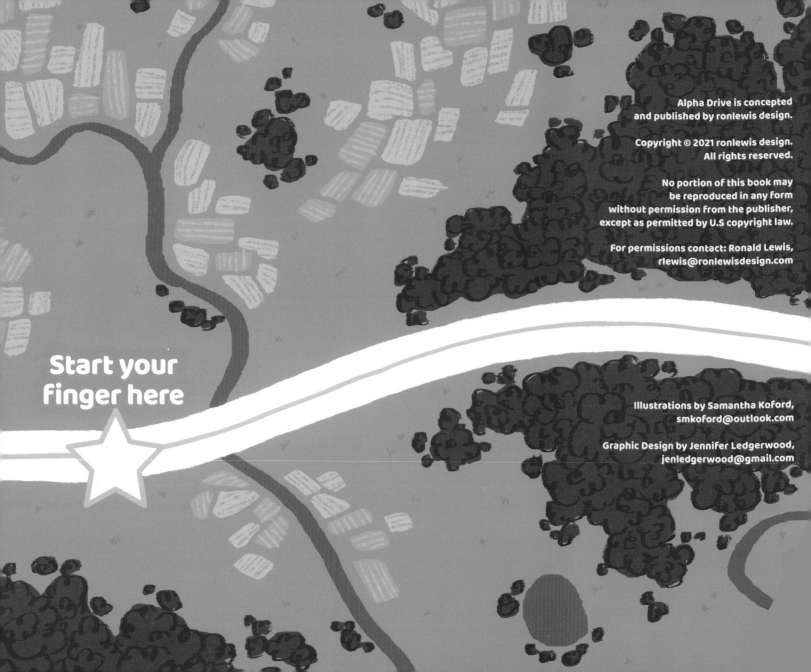

Start your finger here

Alpha Drive is concepted and published by ronlewis design.

For permissions contact: Ronald Lewis, rlewis@ronlewisdesign.com

Illustrations by Samantha Koford, smkoford@outlook.com

Graphic Design by Jennifer Ledgerwood, jenledgerwood@gmail.com

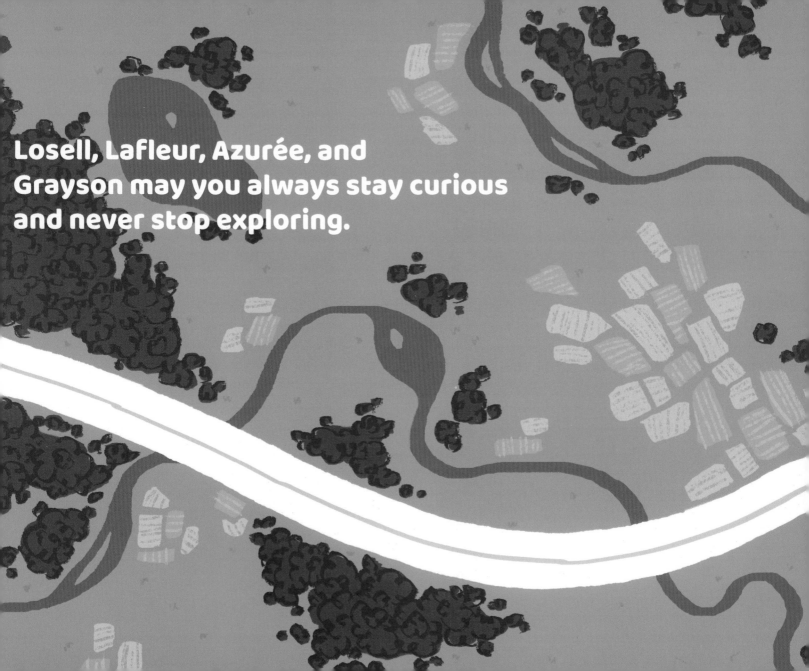

Losell, Lafleur, Azurée, and Grayson may you always stay curious and never stop exploring.

A a airplane

Bb boat

C c cabin

Dd dinosaur

E e eagle

F f fountain

G g garage

H h horse

Jj jungle

K k kite

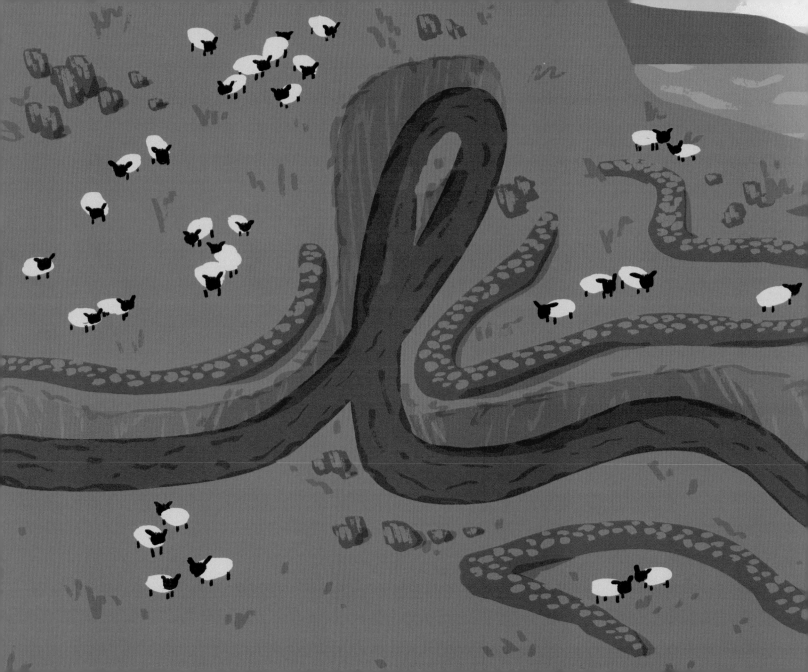

L l lighthouse

Mm mountain

Oo octopus

P p park

R r rocket

T t train

U u umbrella

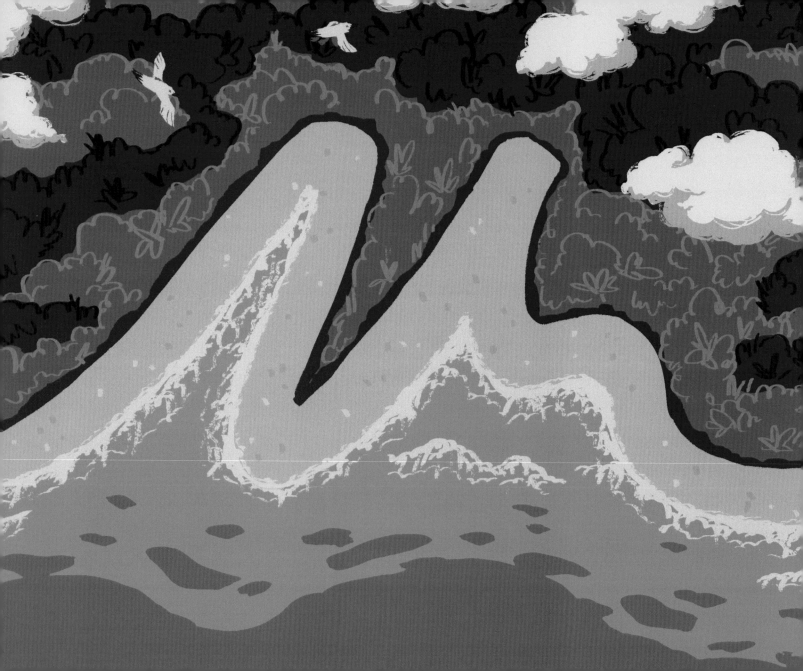

Vv volcano

Ww winter

X x xylophone

Y y yoga

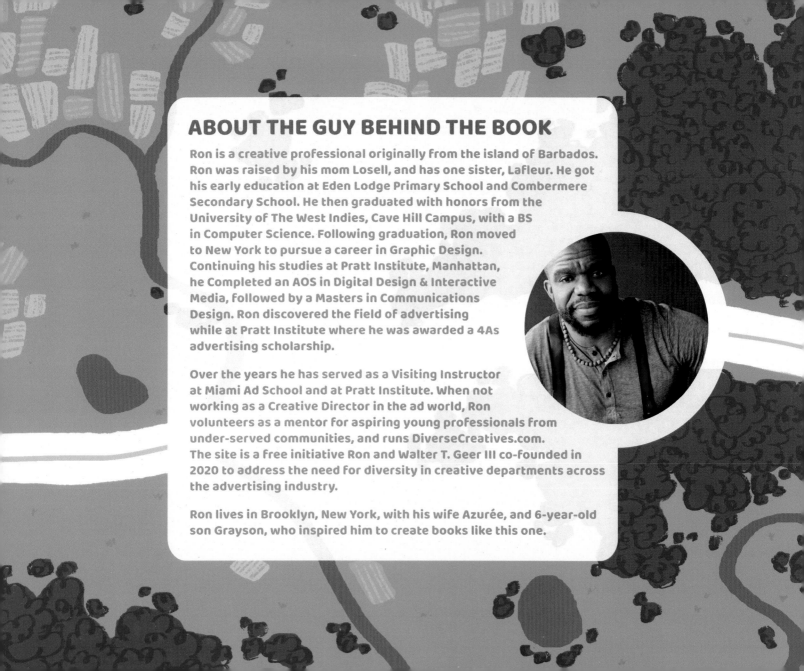

ABOUT THE GUY BEHIND THE BOOK

Ron is a creative professional originally from the island of Barbados. Ron was raised by his mom Losell, and has one sister, Lafleur. He got his early education at Eden Lodge Primary School and Combermere Secondary School. He then graduated with honors from the University of The West Indies, Cave Hill Campus, with a BS in Computer Science. Following graduation, Ron moved to New York to pursue a career in Graphic Design. Continuing his studies at Pratt Institute, Manhattan, he Completed an AOS in Digital Design & Interactive Media, followed by a Masters in Communications Design. Ron discovered the field of advertising while at Pratt Institute where he was awarded a 4As advertising scholarship.

Over the years he has served as a Visiting Instructor at Miami Ad School and at Pratt Institute. When not working as a Creative Director in the ad world, Ron volunteers as a mentor for aspiring young professionals from under-served communities, and runs DiverseCreatives.com. The site is a free initiative Ron and Walter T. Geer III co-founded in 2020 to address the need for diversity in creative departments across the advertising industry.

Ron lives in Brooklyn, New York, with his wife Azurée, and 6-year-old son Grayson, who inspired him to create books like this one.